21st
Century
Skills Library

ROAD TO RECOVERY

MONGOLIAN WILD HORSE

Susan H. Gray

Cherry Lake Publishing
Ann Arbor, Michigan

Published in the United States of America by Cherry Lake Publishing
Ann Arbor, MI
www.cherrylakepublishing.com

Content Adviser: Professor Sue McDonnell, Head, Equine Behavior Lab, University
of Pennsylvania School of Veterinary Medicine, New Bolton Center, Kennett Square,
Pennsylvania

Photo Credits: Page 4, Art Wolfe/The Image Bank/Getty Images; page 5, © Dean Conger/
Corbis; page 7, © Hamid Sardar/Corbis; page 14, © The Gallery Collection/Corbis; page
18, © Lucky Oliver/Steve Cukrov

Maps by XNR Productions, Inc.

Library of Congress Cataloging-in-Publication Data
Gray, Susan Heinrichs.
 Mongolian wild horse / by Susan H. Gray.
    p. cm.—(Road to recovery)
 ISBN-13: 978-1-60279-041-4 (hardcover)
 ISBN-10: 1-60279-041-8 (hardcover)
 1. Przewalski's horse. I. Title. II. Series.
 QL737.U62G73 2007
 599.665'5—dc22   2007004437

Cherry Lake Publishing would like to acknowledge the work of
The Partnership for 21st Century Skills.
Please visit www.21stcenturyskills.org *for more information.*

TABLE OF CONTENTS

CHAPTER ONE

QUIET TIME

Mongolian wild horses graze in a field.

It is a peaceful afternoon, and some of the Mongolian wild horses are

dozing. Others are quietly nibbling the grass. Two horses stand off alone,

side by side, nose to tail. Each one gently nuzzles the coat of the other.

Horses have been important to the Mongolian culture for thousands of years.

21st Century Content

Mongolia is one of Asia's largest countries. It is located between Russia and China. The people are called Mongols. Mongols respect all horses, but one in particular is special to them. It is the small Mongolian wild horse. "We Mongols respect the horse as our companion of night and day . . . and we are nothing without our horses," explains a herdsman in Mongolia.

The snows have melted, and the weather is finally warming up. Horses are starting to shed their thick winter coats. The two horses are grooming each other. They are gently pulling away the old, thick hair.

The Mongolian wild horse's coat protects it from heat in the summer and cold in the winter.

CHAPTER TWO

THE LITTLE HORSE OF MONGOLIA

Two Mongol girls ride horses in a race.

The Mongolian wild horse goes by several names. It is sometimes called Przewalski's (pronounced she-VOL-skeez) horse. The name comes from Nicolai Przhevalsky, a Russian explorer and naturalist who may have first described the animal in 1879. *Przewalski* is the Polish spelling of his name. In Mongolia, people call the Mongolian wild horse the *takh*, a word that means "spirit."

The Mongolian wild horse's unique mane is short and stands straight up.

The takh is small compared to other horses. It is only 48 to 56 inches (122 to 142 centimeters) high at the shoulder. It has a large head, a thick neck, and a stocky body. Its coat can be brownish gray, light red, yellow, or tan. Its chest and belly are lighter in color, sometimes even white. During the winter, the coat is thick and shaggy. Its long winter coat is shed in the spring.

Przewalski's horse has a stiff, dark brown or black mane. This mane stands straight up like a Mohawk haircut. Unlike most other horses, it has no forelock. A dark stripe runs down the animal's back, almost to the tail. A takh's tail and legs are darker than the rest of its body. Some horses have striped legs.

Mongolian wild horses travel in herds. Herds are made up of smaller groups called bands. There are two kinds of bands—family bands and

*Two male Mongolian wild horses fight to win
leadership over the family band.*

bachelor bands. A family band has one adult male, or stallion. It also

includes some mares and their young.

When young females, or fillies, are about two years old, they leave and join other family groups. When young males, or colts, are about two, they leave their family band to join a bachelor band.

In some cases, a bachelor starts his own family. Fillies join the bachelor, and together they form a new band. Such a family group can have up to 20 horses.

Sometimes, a male breaks away from his bachelor band and challenges a stallion in a family band. He tries to take over the stallion's family. The younger horse and the stallion often fight until one wins control of the mares. They bite and kick each other until one is forced to leave. There are plenty of mates for the winning horse. All other adults in the family band are females.

Babies, or foals, are born in the spring or early summer. Within an hour of its birth, the little foal begins to stand up and walk around. At

Mongolian wild horses are members of the horse family. Donkeys, zebras, and common horses are some of the other members. All have long heads and muscular necks. Their bodies are covered with hair. Most have a mane—a strip of long hair that runs down the back of the neck. Horses usually travel in herds. They are swift runners with slender legs and hooves. All are plant-eating animals. Horses live in North, Central, and South America. They also are found in Africa, Europe, Asia, Australia, and even the Arctic.

A mare protects her colt lying in the hot sun.

first, its only food is its mother's milk. After a few weeks, it begins to eat the same food that grown-up horses eat. They eat mainly grass, leaves, and bark.

Sometimes the horses also eat fruit and wild

tulip bulbs.

In the wild, wolves are the natural enemy of

the horses, usually preying on very young foals.

However, Mongolian wild horses know just how to

deal with them. When a wolf comes near a family

band, the mares round up their young. They form

a circle around the little foals. The stallion trots

around the group, guarding his family. He may even

charge at the wolf and run it off.

When Mongolian wild horses travel in a group, they usually walk in single file. In time, they create pathways between feeding places. What does this type of behavior reveal about the Mongolian wild horse?

CHAPTER THREE

A LONG, HARD STORY

Early humans created pictures of horses and other animals on cave walls. This image of a horse that resembles a Mongolian wild horse is in a cave in France.

Mongolian wild horses have quite a history. Some 20,000 years ago,

wild horses roamed throughout Europe and Asia. No one knows for sure whether they were Mongolian wild horses. However, scientists have found

paintings of horses on the walls of caves in Europe. These horses look a lot

like the takh.

Back then, the earth was cooler than it is now. Many horses lived on

cold, grassy plains called steppes. About 10,000 years ago, temperatures

Horses have lived on the harsh Mongolian steppes for thousands of years. Here a traveler sits by a mountain lake in Mongolia.

began to rise. As the earth warmed up, trees began to grow in new areas.

Forests began to replace the steppes. Wild horses had less grass to eat, and

many of them died.

The Mongolian wild horse is the only horse to have never been tamed.

*Some people in Mongolia live in houses they can move so
they can travel with their herds throughout the year.*

The warmer temperatures also made it possible for people to spread

into new areas. People moved into places that had been the takh's home.

They plowed up the grasslands and planted crops. They brought herds of

In the past, Mongolian wild horses lived in the Gobi Desert.

goats, sheep, and cattle. These herds took over in some areas and ate grass

that had been the takh's food. People also hunted the Mongolian wild

horse for food. This went on for centuries.

By 1900, there were very few Mongolian wild horses left. People still saw the horses in the Gobi Desert of China and Mongolia. But their numbers were never very large.

Then things got even worse. People realized the horses were disappearing. So collectors rushed to the Gobi to capture some before they vanished completely. Zoos and large parks sent people to try to catch Mongolian wild horses. Sometimes they killed adult horses that were trying to guard their foals. Captured horses were sent by train or boat to other countries. Many died during the long trips.

Learning & Innovation Skills

Years ago when the Mongolian wild horses were free, they played a big part in nature. Today, the horses are being returned to their natural home. They are again playing an important role.

The horses are plant eaters. They spend much of their time nibbling on grasses, small shrubs, and other plants. As they search for food, they travel several miles each day.

With every meal, the horses take in plant seeds. Quite often, those seeds wind up in the animals' droppings. As the horses wander about, they spread seeds everywhere. New plants spring up, providing more food for the horses. Insects and other animals eat these plants as well. So the horses actually help to feed other animals. How do you think the loss of the Mongolian wild horse would affect other animals in its habitat?

Nonetheless, some horses did survive. Small numbers of takh made it to zoos in Russia, Europe, and North America. Then World War II broke out. When certain large cities were bombed, their zoos were destroyed. So the takh numbers shrank even more. By the end of the war, only 31 Mongolian wild horses were alive in captivity.

By 1970, not a single Mongolian wild horse was living in the Gobi Desert. The only ones left in the world were the few remaining in zoos. The Mongolian wild horse was said to be extinct in the wild.

CHAPTER FOUR

THE ROAD TO RECOVERY

If some Mongolian wild horses had not been in captivity, they would have become extinct.

In 1945, there were only 31 Mongolian wild horses living in zoos around the world. In 1947, one more horse was captured in the wild. This made a total of 32 horses in captivity. Unfortunately, less than half were able to mate and have babies. The takh's future looked bleak.

So animal experts, scientists, and zoo officials got busy with plans to help the takh. Zoo workers began to pay special attention to their Mongolian wild horses. They gave them extra care. They made sure that newborns had everything they needed. Slowly, the numbers began to rise.

In 1960, there were 59 horses living in zoos around the world. However, some had given birth to weak or sickly babies. This can happen when a foal's parents are too closely related.

A scientist in Europe wanted to know how all 59 horses were related to each other. He was curious about which horses were brothers and sisters and which ones were distant cousins. He knew that distant relatives would have the healthiest babies. So he began to draw up a family tree.

Once the family tree was completed, zoos tried something new. They began to trade their horses. Males from some zoos came to mate with females at other zoos. As a result, more and more healthy babies were born. Today, about 2,000 Mongolian wild horses live in captivity, and their whole family tree is on a computer!

A captive breeding program was the Mongolian wild horses' only hope for survival.

21st Century Content

Genghis Khan is one of the great heroes of Mongolia. He was a fierce warrior who lived about 800 years ago. He and his men rode horses that were strong, fast, and very brave. Many people believe Genghis Khan and his men rode Przewalski's horses.

It's great news that there are now so many of these horses in zoos. But the real goal is to get them back in the wild. Experts always knew this would pose problems. They worried that the animals had stayed too long in zoos. They wondered if Przewalski's horses could survive on their own.

In 1992, the horses got a chance to try. That year, zoo horses were released into reserves in Mongolia. Some went to reserves on the steppes and others to reserves in the Gobi Desert. It was a test to see if they could survive.

It was tough for the horses. Wolves killed some of them, and others got sick. But overall, the test was

24

Scientists were uncertain whether Mongolian wild horses could survive in their natural habitat after being raised in captivity.

successful. The Mongolian wild horses proved they

could make it. In time, they were taken from the

reserves and released into the wild.

CHAPTER FIVE

THE TAKH TODAY

In 1960, the situation for the takh was grim. The horse was almost

extinct. Today, it is endangered, but its numbers are growing.

*The Mongolian wild horse population continues to grow,
but the animal is still considered endangered.*

In 2000, experts found that the horses were doing well in Mongolia. Many horses were living in reserves, waiting to be released into the wild. Several others were already running free on the steppes and in the desert.

Although things are better for the takh, problems still arise. Experts argue about where to let the horses go—in the desert or on the steppes. Some say the desert is too hot and dry for them. Others say the steppes are no good because too many people and other animals live there.

Everyone agrees on one very important thing. The Mongolian people themselves must help the wild horse survive. Mongols who own sheep and

21st Century Content

The Gobi Desert covers much of Mongolia. The Gobi B Reserve lies in the southwestern part of the desert. This area gets little rain. Sandstorms often darken the skies. Winters are freezing cold. Nonetheless, Mongolian wild horses are doing well there. They are forming family bands and bachelor bands. New foals are born every year.

The Friends of Takh is a group with members all over the world. The members collaborate with one another to help save the takh. They help to pay the costs of getting the takh back into the wild. They pay for each animal's trip from a European zoo to Mongolia. They also buy feed for the horses and pay for veterinary care. Schoolchildren are even part of the effort to help the animal survive.

goats must share grassy areas with the horses. As the numbers of horses, sheep, goats, and humans increase, people must find new ways to feed them all. They must do this without hunting the takh. It will take a lot of work. But for the Mongolian wild horse, the future looks bright.

Mongolian wild horses are once again living in the wild.

Current range of Mongolian wild horse

This maps shows where the Mongolian wild horse, also called Przewalski's horse, lives in Mongolia.

GLOSSARY

bachelor (BATCH-uh-lur) a mature male horse that has not established his own family band

captivity (kap-TIH-vih-tee) the condition of not being able to roam freely

endangered (en-DAYN-jurd) in danger of dying out completely

extinct (ek-STINGT) no longer living

forelock (FORE-lok) the tuft of hair that falls over the forehead of most horses

herdsman (HURDZ-muhn) someone who owns or breeds farm animals such as horses, cattle, goats, or sheep

mares (MEHRZ) mature female horses

Mongols (MONG-guhlz) people who live in Mongolia

preying (PRAY-ing) eating another animal

reserves (ree-ZURVZ) places set aside for the protection of animals

steppes (STEPS) cold, grassy plains

FOR MORE INFORMATION

Books

Budd, Jackie. *The World of Horses*. Boston: Kingfisher, 2004.

Funston, Sylvia. *The Kids' Horse Book*. Toronto: Maple Tress Press, 2004.

Ransford, Sandy. *The Kingfisher Illustrated Horse and Pony Encyclopedia*. Boston: Kingfisher, 2004.

Web Sites

Foundation for the Preservation and Protection of the Przewalski Horse
www.treemail.nl/takh/index.htm
For information on efforts to save the Mongolian wild horse

Hustai National Park: Takhi
www.owc.org.mn/macne/hustai/Takhi.htm
To read a profile of Mongolian wild horses and information
on Hustai National Park, where they live

INDEX

ABOUT THE AUTHOR

Susan H. Gray has a master's degree in zoology. She has written more than 70 science and reference books for children and especially loves writing about animals. Gray also likes to garden and play the piano. She lives in Cabot, Arkansas, with her husband, Michael, and many pets.